Now I Believe!

WHITE
TREE
PUBLISHING

Now I Believe!

Harry Ironside
(1876-1951)

This White Tree Publishing edition of
"A Selection from the Writing of Harry Ironside
on Assurance."
©White Tree Publishing 2022

This Paperback: ISBN: 978-1-913950-98-9

Also available as an eBook from most distributors
ISBN: 978-1-913950-97-2

Published by
White Tree Publishing
Bristol
UNITED KINGDOM
More books on https://whitetreepublishing.com/

Contact : wtpbristol@gmail.com

Scripture quotations from New American Standard Bible®,
Copyright © 1960, 1971, 1977, 1995 by The Lockman Foundation.
All rights reserved.

Cover image AdobeStock 47252748

Contents

About the Author

Harry (Henry Allen) Ironside has to be one of the greatest Bible teachers in the late nineteenth and first half of the twentieth century. He was born in Toronto, Canada, in 1876 to Christian parents who were great outdoor evangelists. He almost died at birth, because the nurse thought he was dead, and his mother needed major attention. Fortunately, a pulse was subsequently detected and the baby was revived. Sadly, Harry's father died when he was only two years old.

Harry considered himself religious but, as he later came to understand it, he was not a true Christian. However, by the time he was in his early teens he had read the whole Bible fourteen times, and never questioned his standing with God.

When moving from Toronto to Los Angeles, "religious Harry" decided to start his own Sunday school at the age of eleven. In 1888 DL Moody came to preach, and Harry wondered if he would ever preach the crowds like the ones that Moody drew.

In 1889 Harry met the evangelist Donald Munro. One of the first things Donald asked Harry was if he was born again. Harry's uncle Allen tried to defend the boy by explaining that he ran a popular Sunday school, but Munro saw straight through Harry's "religion". For six months Harry struggled with understanding a personal faith, until one night he fell down and said, "Lord, save me."

He expected to feel some special emotion, but instead he realized he had to rely on God's promises. This concern about feelings comes through very much in this book where Harry assures the readers that it is trust, not feelings that we need be concerned about.

Although Harry left school early, he trained to become a lieutenant in the Salvation Army. After leaving the Salvation Army, Harry helped in several street missions, where he met Helen Schofield who became his wife in 1898. He was only twenty-one and had no real income. He and Helen were living by faith.

Early in 1899 Harry and Helen's son, Edmund Henry, was born. Harry continued his mission work, and was soon in much demand because of his clear preaching. Even when he had no formal engagements he would preach on the street corners, even though he and his family could only look in faith for financial help.

Harry's second son, John Schofield, was born in 1905. By this time Harry was already writing books, and he became what can only be described as one of the most prolific Christian authors of all time.

When Harry wasn't writing, he was preaching. As he says in Chapter 1 of this book, he travelled thirty to forty thousand miles a year. Not only did Harry preach in America, but in 1936 he went to Palestine and then to Britain. He travelled to Britain again in the three following years, where he was much in demand. His wife Helen died in 1948, soon after she and Harry celebrated their Golden Wedding.

By 1949 Harry's eyesight was failing, and he retired to Indiana where he married Annie Turner Hightower. She was a great help to him with his failing eyesight, but an operation eventually put that right and he set out to see his sister in New Zealand in 1950 on a planned preaching tour, but he died soon after arriving. Before his death he requested that he would be buried there where his sister lived.

Estimates of his publications vary between sixty and ninety, depending on whether only bound printed books are included. It is indeed possible to see why Harry (Henry Allen) Ironside has to be one of the greatest teachers of the Bible in the late eighteenth and first half of the twentieth century.

Publisher's Introduction

Harry Ironside was indeed a great writer, and he is able to put a finger on exactly the points that concern us regarding our Christian faith. For this book, we have edited and abridged sections from Harry's book on "Full Assurance" which was one of a series originally published by Moody Press in the Moody Colportage Library series as inexpensive paperbacks in the 1920s and 30s, for distribution by street preachers and churches.

These little books were extremely popular, but of a fixed length. Looking at "Full Assurance" today, there seems to have been a considerable amount of extra material added in order to reach the required length. Or maybe it was the right length for readers at the time, but in these busy days we feel it is essential that only the most important and memorable parts of Harry's writing should be shown here.

In common with many Christian writers from this period, there seems to be an assumption that the reader will know exactly where to find a quoted verse, or one referred to. In this book we have made sure that every single quoted verse, and every referral to a verse, is given the full Scripture reference. We hope that readers will look up these verses in their own Bible.

In this White Tree Publishing edition, apart from keeping a quotation from the Twenty-Third Psalm in the KJV, we have changed the King James Version to that of the modern NASB translation, which uses words which many readers today will find easier to understand.

If you do not have access to a printed Bible (and you may want to read the passages in a different version anyway) you can find free online Bibles of nearly every English version, old and new, on the Bible App you can download at https://www.youversion.com/ or find by entering "youversion" in the Apple and Android app stores.

On the youversion website you will find Bible readings with helpful notes for every day of the year, plus other Bible related material. There are also Bible versions in many other languages, all free.

We aim to make our eBooks free or for a nominal cost, and cannot invest in other forms of advertising. However, word of mouth by satisfied readers will also help get our books more widely known. When the book finishes, please take a look at our website for other books we publish: Christian non-fiction, Christian fiction, and books for younger readers – a range of over 200 books available from White Tree Publishing. More details on our website :

https://whitetreepublishing.com/

PART ONE

Chapter 1

Doubts

I have only one outstanding object before me: to make as plain as I possibly can just how any troubled soul can find settled peace with God. I am thinking particularly of those people who believe the Holy Scriptures to be divinely inspired, and who recognize that salvation is only to be found in Jesus Christ, but have somehow missed the "peace of a perfect trust." Though sincerely wanting to know the Lord, they are floundering in confusion.

Consequently, no attempt is made here to prove that the Bible is true, as both the writer and the readers he has chiefly in view take that for granted. People who are bothered by doubts along that line will find plenty of help elsewhere. There is no lack of good books written by sound Christian scholars who present unanswerable arguments for the inerrancy and the divine authority of the Bible.

The trouble is that so many people who profess to want help along these lines are too lazy to investigate, even when the opportunity is put before them. It is to the really earnest seekers after the truth that I am writing.

For most of my life I have been an itinerant preacher of the gospel, travelling often as much as thirty to forty thousand miles a year to proclaim the unsearchable riches of Jesus Christ. In all these years I only recall two occasions on which I have missed my trains. One was by becoming confused between what is known as daylight saving and standard time.

The other was through the passive assurance of a farmer-host, who was to drive me from his country home into the town of Lowry, Minnesota, in time for me to take an afternoon train for Winnipeg, on which I had a Pullman reservation. I can remember how I urged my friend to get on the way, but he pottered about with all kinds of inconsequential chores, insisting that there was plenty of time. I fumed and fretted to no purpose. He was calmly adamant.

Finally, he hitched up his team and we started across the prairie. About a mile from town we saw the train steam into the station, pause a few moments, and depart for the north. There was nothing to do but wait some five or six hours for the night express, on which I had no reservation, and when it arrived I found I could not get a berth, so was obliged to sit in a crowded day coach all the way to the Canadian border, after which there was more room.

While annoyed, I comforted myself with the words, *"And we know that God causes all things to work together for good to those who love God, to those who are called according to His purpose"* (Romans 8:28). I prayed earnestly that if He had some purpose in permitting me to miss my train and comfortable accommodations, I might not fail to find it out.

When I boarded the crowded coach, I found there was only one vacancy left and that was half of a seat midway down the car, a sleeping young man occupying the other half. As I sat down by him and stowed away my baggage, he awoke, straightened up, and gave me a rather sleepy greeting. Soon we were in an agreeable, low-toned conversation, while other passengers slept and snored all about us.

A suitable opportunity presenting itself, I inquired, "Do you know the Lord Jesus Christ?" He sat up as though shot. "How strange that you should ask me that! I went to sleep thinking of Him and wishing I did know Him, but I do not understand, though I want to! Can you help me?"

Further conversation revealed the fact that he had been working in a town in southern Minnesota, where he had been persuaded to attend some revival meetings. Evidently, the preaching was in power and he became deeply concerned about his soul. He had even gone forward to the mourners' bench, but though he wept and prayed over his sins, he came away without finding peace.

I knew then why I had missed my train. This was my Gaza, and though unworthy I was sent by God to be His Philip (Acts 8:27-38). So I opened my Bible to the same Scripture that the Ethiopian treasurer had been reading when Philip met him: Isaiah 53.

Drawing my newly-found friend's attention to its wonderful depiction of the crucified Savior, though written seven hundred years before the event, I showed him verses 4, 5 and 6: "*Surely our griefs He Himself bore, and our sorrows He carried; yet we ourselves esteemed Him stricken, smitten of God, and afflicted. But He was pierced through for our transgressions, He was crushed for our iniquities; the chastening for our well-being fell upon Him, and by His scourging we are healed. All of us like sheep have gone astray, each of us has turned to his own way; but the Lord has caused the iniquity of us all to fall on Him."*

As the young man read them, the truths seemed to burn their way into his very soul. He saw himself as the lost sheep that had gone its own way. He saw Jesus as the One on whom Jehovah laid all his iniquity, and he bowed his head and told Him he would trust Him as his own Savior.

For perhaps two hours we had hallowed fellowship on the way, as we turned from one Scripture to another. Then he reached his destination and left, thanking me most profusely for showing him the way of life. I have never seen him since, but I know I will greet him again at the judgment seat of Christ.

Into whose hands this book will fall I cannot tell, but I send it out with the prayer that it may prove as timely a message to many a needy soul as the talk on the train that night in Minnesota with the young man who felt his need and had really turned to God. But he did not understand the way of peace and so had no assurance – until he found it through the written Word, borne home to his soul in the power of the Holy Spirit.

If you are just as troubled as that young man, and should by divine providence read this short book at any time, I trust that you will see that it is the Lord's own way of seeking to draw you to Himself, and that you will read it carefully, thoughtfully, and prayerfully, looking up each passage referred to in your own Bible if you have one, and that thus you, too, can obtain full assurance.

Be certain of this: God is deeply concerned about you. He longs to give you the knowledge of His salvation. It is no mere accident that these pages have come to your attention. He put it on my heart to write them. He would have you read them. They may prove to be His own message to your troubled soul. God's ways are varied. But, *"God so loved the world, that He gave His only begotten Son, that whoever believes in Him shall not perish, but have eternal life."* (John 3:16).

Another personal experience will perhaps highlight and fittingly close this chapter. One afternoon I was walking the busy streets of Indianapolis, looking for a barber shop. Entering the first one I saw, I was soon seated in the chair, and the barber began operations.

He was chatty but subdued, I thought, not carelessly voluble. Praying for an opening, it soon seemed a fitting time to ask, as in the other case, "Are you acquainted with the Lord Jesus Christ?"

To my astonishment, the barber's reaction was remarkable. He stopped his work, burst into uncontrollable weeping. When the first outburst had passed, he exclaimed, "How strange that you should ask me about Him! In all my life I never had a man ask me that before. I have been thinking of Him nearly all the time for the last three days. What can you tell me about Him?"

It was my turn to be amazed. I asked him what had led up to this. He explained that he had gone to see the film of a Passion Play, and that it had made an indelible impression on his mind. He kept asking, "Why did that good Man have to suffer so? Why did God let Him die like that?" He had never heard the gospel in his life, so I spent an hour with him opening up the story of the Cross.

We prayed together and he declared that all was

now plain, and he trusted the Savior for himself. I had the joy of knowing, as I left his shop, that the gospel was indeed the power of God to salvation to him, an uninstructed Greek barber, who had learned for the first time that Jesus loved him and gave Himself for him.

To me it was a wonderful instance of divine sovereignty. The very idea of that film – unbelieving men endeavoring to portray the life, death and resurrection of Jesus – was distasteful to me. But, *"Do I have any pleasure in the death of the wicked," declares the Lord God, "rather than that he should turn from his ways and live?"* (Ezekiel 18:23). God used that very film to arouse this man and so make him ready to hear the gospel.

I could not doubt that He had directed my steps to that particular shop, that I might have the joy of pointing the anxious barber to the Lamb of God that takes away the sin of the world (John 1:29).

Chapter 2

Assurance Forever

There is a very remarkable statement found in the book of Isaiah, chapter thirty-two, verse 17: *"And the work of righteousness will be peace, and the service of righteousness, quietness and confidence forever."*

Peace, quietness, confidence – forever. Assurance forever! Assurance not for a few days, or weeks, or months – nor yet for a few years, or even a lifetime – but *forever*! It is this blessed assurance that God delights to give to all who come to Him as needy sinners seeking the way of life.

How many deeply religious people there are in the world who scarcely know the meaning of these words. They are honestly seeking God. They are meticulous about their religious duties, such as reading the Scriptures, saying their prayers, attending church, partaking of the sacrament, and supporting the cause of Christ.

They are scrupulously honest and upright in all their dealings with others, endeavoring to fulfill every civic and national responsibility, and to obey the golden rule. Yet they have no lasting peace, nor any definite assurance of salvation. I am persuaded that in practically every such instance the reason for their unquiet and unsettled state is due to a lack of understanding of God's way of salvation.

Though living seven centuries before Calvary, it was

given to Isaiah to set out in a very clear way the right-eousness of God as later revealed in the gospel. This is not to be wondered at, for he spoke as he was moved by the Holy Spirit.

The bodily resurrection of Jesus is the divine token that all has been dealt with to God's satisfaction. Jesus bore our sins on the cross. He made Himself responsible for them. He died to put them away forever. But God raised Him from the dead, thereby attesting His good pleasure in the work of His Son.

Now the blessed Lord sits exalted at the right hand of the Majesty in the heavens. He could not be there if our sins were still upon Him. The fact that He is there proves that they are completely put away. God is satisfied!

It is this that gives quietness and assurance forever. When I know that my sins have been dealt with in such a way that God's righteousness remains untarnished, even as He folds me to His bosom, a justified believer, I have perfect peace. I know Him now as "*a righteous God and a Savior*" (Isaiah 45:21).

He says, "*I bring near My righteousness, it is not far off; and My salvation will not delay*" (Isaiah 46:13). What cheering words are these! God has provided a righteousness – His very own, for people who have none of their own! Gladly, therefore, do I spurn all attempts at self-righteousness, so as to be found in Him perfect and complete, clothed with *His* righteousness.

Every believer can say with the prophet Isaiah, "*I will rejoice greatly in the Lord, My soul will exult in my God; For He has clothed me with garments of salvation, He has wrapped me with a robe of right-eousness, As a bridegroom decks himself with a garland, And as a bride adorns herself with her jewels"* (Isaiah 61:10).

> "Clad in this robe, how bright I shine;
> Angels have not a robe like mine."

It is given only to redeemed sinners to wear this garment of glory. Jesus Christ Himself is the robe of righteousness. We who trust Him are "in Christ"; so that, *"we might become the righteousness of God in Him"* (2 Corinthians 5:21), *"who became to us wisdom from God, and righteousness and sanctification, and redemption"* (1 Corinthians 1:30).

If my acceptance depended on my growth in grace I could never have settled peace. It would be arrogance of the worst kind to consider myself so holy that I could be acceptable to God on the ground of my personal life. But when I see it is *"to the praise of the glory of His grace, which He freely bestowed on us in the Beloved"* (Ephesians 1:6), every doubt is banished. My soul is at peace. I have quietness and assurance forever.

As long as these great unchanging truths remain, my peace is unshaken, my confidence is secure. Do you not see it? Can you not rest where God rests, in the finished work of His blessed Son? If He is satisfied to save you by faith in Jesus, surely you should be satisfied to trust Him.

An aged woman was reported to be dying. Her physician had given up all hope of her recovery. Her minister was called to her bedside to prepare her for the great change. She was in much distress. Bitterly she lamented her sins, her coldness of heart, her feeble efforts to serve the Lord. Piteously she besought her pastor to give what help he could, that dying grace might indeed be hers.

The good man was plainly disconcerted. He was not used to coming to close quarters with dying souls anxious to be sure of salvation. But he quoted and read various Scriptures. His eye fell on the words, *"He saved us, not on the basis of deeds which we have done in righteousness, but according to His mercy, by the washing of regeneration and renewing by the Holy Spirit, whom He poured out upon us richly through Jesus Christ our Savior, so that being justified by His grace we would be made heirs according to the hope of eternal life"* (Titus 3:5-7).

As he read the words with quivering voice, the dying woman drank in their truth. "Not by what we have done, but justified by His grace!" she exclaimed, "Aye, minister, that'll do. I can rest there. No works of mine to plead, just to trust His grace. That will do. I can die in peace."

He prayed with her and left, his own heart tenderly moved and grateful, too, that he had been used to minister dying grace to this troubled member of his flock. He hardly expected to see her again on earth, but was comforted to feel that she would soon be in heaven.

Contrary to her physician's prediction, however, she did not die but rallied from that very hour, and in a few weeks was well again, a happy, rejoicing believer with much assurance.

She sent once more for the pastor, and put the strange question to him: "God has given me dying grace and now I am well again. What am I to do about it?"

"Ah," he exclaimed, "you can just claim it as living grace and abide in the joy of it."

It was well put, but what a pity his preaching throughout the years had not produced assurance long before in the mind and heart of his anxious parishioner.

It is a great mistake to attempt to rest one's soul on the character of any preachers, however godly they may appear to be. Faith is to rest, not in the best of God's servants but in His unchanging Word. Unhappily, it often transpires that impressionable folk are carried away with admiration for a minister of Christ, and they put their dependence on him, rather than on the truth proclaimed.

"I was converted by Billy Sunday himself!" someone once said to me, in answer to the question, "Are you certain that your soul is saved?"

[Billy Sunday was a famous baseball player and preacher in the late 1800s.]

Mr. Sunday would have been the last of men to put himself in the place of Jesus. Further conversation seemed to bring out the evidence that the person in question had been carried away by admiration for the earnest evangelist, and mistook the "thrill of a handshake" for the Spirit's witness. At least, there seemed no real understanding of God's plan of salvation, which Billy Sunday preached in such tremendous power.

Then it is well to remember that some vivid emotional experience is not a safe ground of assurance. It is the blood of Jesus that makes us safe – and the Word of God that makes us sure.

When Israel of old were about to leave Egypt, and the last awful plague was to fall on that land and its people, God Himself provided a way of escape for His own. They were to slay a lamb, sprinkle its blood on the doorposts and lintel of their houses, go inside and shut

17

the door.

When the destroying angel passed through that night, he would not be permitted to enter any blood-sprinkled door, for Jehovah had said, "When I see the blood, I will pass over you."

Inside the house, some might have been trembling and some rejoicing, but all were safe. Their security depended, not on their state of mind, or feelings, but on the fact that the eye of God saw the blood of the lamb and they were sheltered behind it. As they recalled the Word that He had given concerning it, and truly believed it, they would have much assurance.

So it is today! We cannot see the blood shed so long ago for our redemption on Calvary, but there is a sense in which it is ever before the eye of God. The moment a repentant sinner puts their trust in Jesus Christ, they are viewed by God as sheltered behind the blood-sprinkled lintel.

Imagine a Jewish youth on that night in Egypt reasoning thus: "I'm the first-born of this family and in thousands of homes tonight the first-born must die. I wish I could be sure that I'm safe and secure, but when I think of my many shortcomings, I am in deepest distress and perplexity. I do not feel that I'm by any means good enough to be saved when others must die. I have been very willful, very disobedient, very undependable, and now I feel so troubled and anxious. I question very much if I will see the morning light."

Would his anxiety and self-condemnation leave him exposed to judgment? Surely not! His father might well say to him, "Son, what you say as to yourself is all true. Not one of us has ever been all we should be. We all deserve to die. But the death of the lamb was for you –

the lamb died in your stead. The blood of the lamb outside the house comes between you and the destroyer."

One can understand how the young man's face would light up as he exclaimed, "Ah, I see it! It is not what I *am* that saves me from judgment. It is the *blood*, and I am safe behind the blood-sprinkled door."

Thus he would have "much assurance." And in the same way, we now, who trust in the testimony God has given concerning the atoning work of His Son, enter into peace and know we are free from all condemnation.

Perhaps someone asks, "But does it make no difference to God what I am myself? Can I live on in my sins and still be saved?" No, assuredly not! But this brings in another line of truth. The moment someone believes the gospel, they are born again and they receive a new life and nature – a nature that hates sin and loves holiness.

If you have come to Jesus and trusted Him, do you not realize the truth of this? Do you not now hate and detest the wrong things that once gave you a certain degree of delight? Do you not find within yourself a new craving for goodness, a longing after holiness, and a thirst for righteousness? All this is the evidence of a new nature. And as you walk with God you will find that daily the power of the indwelling Holy Spirit will give you practical deliverance from the dominion of sin.

This line of truth does not touch the *validity* of your salvation. It is the *outcome* of your salvation. First, get this settled: you are *justified* not by anything done in you, but by what Jesus did for you on the cross.

Acceptable service springs from the knowledge that

the question of salvation is settled for ever. We who are saved by grace, apart from all self effort, are "*His workmanship, created in Christ Jesus for good works, which God prepared beforehand so that we would walk in them*" (Ephesians 2:10).

Notice, we are not saved *by* good works, but *for* good works. In other words, no one can begin to live a Christian life until they have a Christian life to live. This life is divine and eternal. It is imparted by God Himself to the one who believes the gospel – the Good News of salvation.

The apostle Peter tells us: "*You have been born again not of seed which is perishable but imperishable, that is, through the living and enduring word of God. For, 'All flesh is like grass, And all its glory like the flower of grass. The grass withers, and the flower falls off, but the word of the Lord endures forever.' And this is the word which was preached to you*" (1 Peter 1:23-25).

The new birth, therefore, is by the Word – the message of the gospel – and the power of the Holy Spirit. "*That which is born of the flesh is flesh, and that which is born of the Spirit is spirit*" (John 3:6). These were our Lord's words to Nicodemus. The one thus regenerated has eternal life and can never perish. How do we know? Because He has told us so!

Weigh carefully the precious words of John 5:24. "*Truly, truly, I say to you, he who hears My word, and believes Him who sent Me, has eternal life, and does not come into judgment, but has passed out of death into life*".

And now link that verse with these words, John 10:27-30, "*My sheep hear My voice, and I know them, and they follow Me; and I give eternal life to them, and they will never perish; and no one will snatch them out of My hand. My Father, who has given them to Me, is greater than all; and no one is able to snatch them out of the Father's hand. I and the Father are one."*

Observe that in the first of these passages there are five links, all of which go together: "Hears" – "Believes" – "Has" – "Will never" – "Has passed." Consider these terms carefully and note their true connection. They should never be separated. In the second passage pay careful attention to what is said of Jesus Christ's sheep:

a – They hear His voice;
b – They follow Him;
c – They possess eternal life;
d – They will never perish;
e – No one can snatch them out of Jesus' hand – or out of the Father's hand. They are One.

Could there be greater security than this, and could any words give clearer assurance of the complete salvation of all who come to God through His Son? To doubt His testimony is to make God a liar. To believe His record is to have "much assurance."

Do you say, "I will *try* to believe"? Try to believe who? Dare you speak in this way of the living God who will never call back His words? Rather look up to Him, confessing all the unbelief of the past as sin, trust Him now, and so know that you are one of the redeemed.

Some years ago in St. Louis, a worker was dealing with a man who had expressed his desire to be saved by going into the inquiry room upon the invitation of the evangelist. The worker endeavored to show the man that the way to be saved was by accepting Jesus as his Savior and believing the promise of God. But the man kept saying: "I can't believe; I can't believe!"

"Who can't you believe?" replied the worker.

"Who can't I believe?" asked the man.

"Yes, *who* can't you believe? Can't you believe God? He cannot lie."

"Why, yes," said the man, "I can believe God; but I had never thought of it in that way before. I thought you had to have some sort of feeling."

The man had been trying to work up a sense of faith, instead of relying on the sure promise of God. For the first time he realized that he had to take God at His word, and as he did so, he experienced the power and assurance of salvation.

Chapter 3

Full Assurance of Faith

In Hebrews 10:19-22, we find the words which we will consider together. Read the entire passage very thoughtfully: *"Therefore, brethren, since we have confidence to enter the holy place by the blood of Jesus, by a new and living way which He inaugurated for us through the veil, that is, His flesh, and since we have a great priest over the house of God, let us draw near with a sincere heart in full assurance of faith, having our hearts sprinkled clean from an evil conscience and our bodies washed with pure water."*

Do you notice that remarkable expression, *"full assurance of faith"*? Does it not thrill your soul as you read it? *"Full assurance!"* What could be more precious? And it is for you if you want it – but you must receive it by faith. Observe carefully, it is not the full assurance of an emotional experience, nor the full assurance of a carefully reasoned out system of philosophy. It is the *full* assurance of *faith*.

The little boy was right who replied to his teacher's question, "What is faith?" by exclaiming, "Faith is believing God and asking no questions." That is exactly what it is. Faith is taking God at His word. This is the real meaning of that wonderful definition given by inspiration in Hebrews 11:1 – *"Now faith is the assurance of things hoped for, the conviction of things not seen."*

God tells us something beyond human understanding. Faith gives substance to it. It makes unseen things even more real than things that the eye beholds. It relies in unquestioning certainty upon what God has declared to be true. And when there is this complete reliance on the promise of God, the Holy Spirit bears witness to the truth, so that the believer has the full assurance of faith.

Faith is not, however, mere intellectual acceptance of certain facts. It involves trust and confidence in those facts, and this results in the word of faith and the work of faith. Faith in Jesus is not, therefore, simply accrediting the historical statements revealed concerning our blessed Lord. It is to trust one's self wholly to Him in reliance on His redemptive work. To believe is to trust. To trust is to have faith. To have faith in Jesus Christ is to have *full* assurance of salvation.

Because this is so, faith must have something tangible to lay hold of, some definite worthwhile message to rest on. And it is just this that is set out in the gospel, which is God's well-ordered plan of salvation for sinners who otherwise are lost, helpless and hopeless.

When we are bidden to draw near to God with true hearts *in full assurance of faith*, the meaning is that we are to rest implicitly on what God has revealed concerning His Son and His glorious work for our redemption. This is set out admirably in the early part of this chapter in Hebrews where our verse is found.

There we have set out in vivid contrast the difference between the many sacrifices offered under the Old Testament legal dispensation, the Old Covenant, and the one perfect, all-sufficient offering and sacrifice of our Lord Jesus Christ – the New Covenant. Note some of the outstanding differences:

1. In the Old Testament, sacrifices were many and often repeated – but Jesus' sacrifice is only one, and no other will ever be required.

2. In the Old Testament, the sacrifices did not have the necessary value to settle the sin question – but Jesus' sacrifice is of such infinite value, it has settled that problem forevermore.

3. In the Old Testament the sacrifices could not purge the consciences of those who brought them – but Jesus' sacrifice cleanses all who believe, giving a perfect conscience because all sin has been put away from under the eye of God.

4. In the Old Testament the sacrifices could not open the way into the Holy of Holies – but Jesus' sacrifice has torn the Temple veil, and brought about the new and living way into the very presence of God.

5. The Old Testament sacrifices could not make perfect the one who offered them – but Jesus' one sacrifice has made perfect forever those who are sanctified.

6. In the Old Testament there was a remembrance again of sins from year to year – but Jesus' sacrifice has enabled God to say, "*I will be merciful to their iniquities, and I will remember their sins no more*" (Hebrews 8:12).

7. In the Old Testament it was not possible that the blood of bulls and of goats could put away sin – but Jesus has accomplished that very thing by the sacrifice of Himself.

Here then is where faith rests – on the *finished* work of Jesus Christ. Yes, His work is finished! It will help us greatly to understand this if we glance at what is revealed concerning the sin offering of the Old Testament dispensation.

Let us imagine that we stand near the altar in the temple court, and a troubled Israelite comes with his sacrifice. He leads a goat along to the place of the offering. The priest examines it carefully, and finding it without any outward blemish he commands it to be slain. It is then cut open, and its inward parts carefully inspected.

Pronounced perfect, it is accepted, and the meat placed on the fire of the altar. The blood is sprinkled round about the altar and on its four horns, after which the priest pronounces absolution, assuring the man of his forgiveness.

This was but "*only a shadow of the good things to come*" (Hebrews 10:1), and could not actually put away sin. That unblemished animal foreshadows the sinless Savior who became the great Sin Offering. His blood has made full and complete payment for iniquity. All who come to God through Him are eternally forgiven.

If the Israelite sinned against the Lord the next day, he was required to bring a new sacrifice. His conscience was never made perfect. But Jesus Christ's one offering is of such infinite value that it settles the sin question eternally – for all who put their trust in Him. "*For by one offering He has perfected for all time those who are sanctified*" (Hebrews 10:14).

To be sanctified in this sense is to be set apart to God in all the value of the atoning work and the personal perfections of Jesus Christ. He is Himself our sanctification. God sees us from now on in His Son.

Is not this a wonderfully precious truth? It is something man would never have dreamed of. God alone devised such a plan. The person who believes His testimony regarding it, has full assurance of faith. We do not know we are saved because we feel happy. But every true believer will be happy to know they are saved.

Confidence based on an emotional experience would leave someone in utter bewilderment when that emotion passed away. But assurance based on the Word of God remains fixed, because His Word is unchangeable.

Many years ago I was holding a series of evangelistic meetings in a little country schoolhouse some miles out of Santa Cruz, California. One day I was out driving with a kindly old gentleman who was attending the services nightly, but who was far from being sure of his personal salvation.

As we drove along a beautiful, winding tree-lined road, I put the definite question to him, "Have you peace with God?" He drew rein at once, stopped the horse, and exclaimed, "Now that's what I brought you here for. I won't go another foot until I know I am saved, or else know it is hopeless to seek to be sure of it."

"How do you expect to find out?" I inquired.

"Well, that is what puzzles me. I want a definite sign. Something that I cannot be mistaken about."

"Just what would you consider definite? Some inward emotional stirring?"

"I can hardly say, only most folks tell us they felt some powerful change when they got religion. I have been seeking that for years, but it has always eluded me."

"Getting religion is one thing; trusting Jesus Christ can be quite another. But now suppose you were seeking salvation, and suddenly there came to you a very happy feeling. Would you be sure then that you were saved?"

"Well, I think I would."

"Then, suppose you went through life resting on that experience, and at last came down to the hour of death. Imagine Satan telling you that you were lost and would soon be beyond hope of mercy. What would you say to him? Would you tell him that you knew all was well, because you had such a happy emotional experience years before? What if he should declare that it was he who gave you that happy feeling, in order to deceive you? Could you prove it was not?"

"No," he answered thoughtfully, "I couldn't. I see that a happy feeling is not enough."

"What would be enough?"

"If I could get some definite word in a vision, or a message from an angel, then I could be sure."

"But suppose you had a vision of a glorious angel, and he told you your sins were forgiven. Would that really be enough to rest on?"

"I think it would. I ought to be certain if an angel said it was all right."

"But if you were dying and Satan was there to disturb you, and told you that you were lost after all, what could you say?"

"Why, I'd tell him an angel told me I was saved."

"But if he said, 'I was that angel. I transformed myself into an angel of light to deceive you. And now you are where I wanted you – you will be lost forever.' What then could you say?"

He pondered a moment or two, and then replied, "I see, you are right. The word of an angel won't do."

"But now," I said, "God has given something better than happy feelings, something more dependable than the voice of an angel. He has given His Son to die for your sins, and He has testified in His own unalterable Word that if you trust in Him, all your sins are gone. Listen to this: '*Of Him all the prophets bear witness that through His name everyone who believes in Him receives forgiveness of sins.*' These are the words of God spoken through His apostle Peter, as recorded in Acts 10:43.

"Then here in 1 John 5:13, it says, '*These things I have written to you who believe in the name of the Son of God, so that you may know that you have eternal life.*' Are these words addressed to you? Do you believe in the Name of the Son of God?"

"I do, sir, I do indeed! I know He is the Son of God, and I know He died for me."

"Then see what He tells you that, '*you may know that you have eternal life.*' Is not this enough to rest on? It is a letter from heaven directed to *you*. How can you refuse to accept what God has told you? Can you not believe Him? Is He not more to be depended on than an angel, or than aroused emotions? Can you not take Him at His word, and rest on it for the forgiveness of your sins?"

After a pause, I continued. "Now suppose that as you are dying, Satan comes to you and insists that you are lost, but you reply, 'No, Satan, you cannot terrify me now. I rest on the Word of the living God and He tells me I have eternal life, and also the forgiveness of all my sins.' Can you not do this now? Will you not bow your head and tell God you will be saved on *His* terms by coming to Him as a repentant sinner, trusting His word concerning His blessed Son?"

The old man dropped his eyes, and I saw that he was deeply stirred. His lips were moving in prayer. Suddenly he looked up and touching the horse lightly with his whip, exclaimed, "Giddup! It's all clear now. This is what I've wanted for years."

That night at the meeting he came to the front and told everyone that what he had sought in vain, for half a lifetime, he had found when he believed the message of God's Word about what Jesus had done to save sinners.

For several years he was a regular correspondent of mine until the Lord took him home – a joyous saint whose doubts and fears had all been banished when he rested on the sure Word of God. His was the full assurance of faith.

Please do not misunderstand me. I do not discount the emotional element in conversion, but I insist it will not do to rely on it as an evidence that one has been forgiven. When someone is awakened by the Spirit of God to realize something of their lost, undone condition, it would be strange indeed if their emotions were not aroused.

When people are brought to repentance, that is, to a complete change of attitude toward their sins, toward themselves, and toward God, we need not be surprised to see the tears of penitence coursing down their cheeks.

When they rest their soul on what God has said, and receive in faith the Spirit's witness, *"I will remember their sins no more"* (Hebrews 8:12), it would be unthinkable but that, like Wesley, their heart should be "strangely warmed" as they rejoice in God's salvation.

What I am trying to make plain is that assurance is

not based on any emotional change. Whatever emotional experience there may be, it will be the result of accepting the testimony of the Lord given in the Scriptures.

Faith rests on the naked Word of God. That Word, when believed, gives full assurance. Then the Holy Spirit comes to dwell in the believers' heart, to conform them to Jesus Christ. Growth in grace follows naturally when the soul has trusted Jesus and entered into peace with God.

As soon as someone knows they are saved, they should begin, in dependence on the Holy Spirit, a careful, regular, systematic study of the Word of God. The Bible is our Father's letter to us, His redeemed children. We should value it as that which reveals His mind, and indicates the way in which He would have us walk.

"All Scripture is inspired by God and profitable for teaching, for reproof, for correction, for training in righteousness; so that the man of God may be adequate, equipped for every good work" (2 Timothy 3:16-17).

The study of the Word will instruct me in the truth. It will show me what needs to be rectified in my life and walk, it will make clear how I can get right with God, and it will guide me in paths of uprightness. No Christian can afford to neglect their Bible. If they do, they will be stunted and dwarfed in their spiritual life, and will be a prey to doubts and fears, and can be carried about by every wind of doctrine.

Chapter 4

Two Members

As newborn babes require milk, so the regenerated soul needs to be nourished on the Word. Many uninstructed believers become discouraged because of their own failures, and Satan takes advantage of these to inject into their minds doubts as to whether they are not deceiving themselves after all in supposing they are Christians. But a knowledge of the truth as to the believer's two natures will often help here.

It is important to understand that sin in the flesh, inherent in the old nature, is not destroyed when someone is born again. On the contrary, that old sin-principal remains in the believer as long as they are in the body. What takes place at new birth is that a new and divine nature is communicated. These two natures are in conflict with each other.

The Christian who walks in the Spirit will not fulfill the desires of the flesh, even though at times those desires can be powerful. In order to so walk, we must take sides with God against this principle of evil which belongs to our old nature of Adam. The Lord Jesus died, not only for what we have done, but for what we are by nature.

Now faith accepts this as true, and the believer can exclaim, "*I have been crucified with Christ; and it is no longer I who live, but Christ lives in me; and the life which I now live in the flesh I live by faith in the Son of God, who loved me and gave Himself up for me*" (Galatians 2:20).

The Lord Jesus said, "*You will know the truth, and the truth will make you free*" (John 8:32). How necessary then for His redeemed ones to study His Word in dependence on His Holy Spirit, that we can be delivered both from the fears that are the result of ignorance of His truth, and the pride that is a result of self-confidence.

The liberating Word alone will give to the honest, yielded souls who approach it prayerfully the full assurance of understanding. For it is written: "*The unfolding of Your words gives light; it gives understanding to the simple*" (Psalm 119:130).

And so as one goes on in the Christian life, and various problems and perplexities arise, it will be found that the Word of God will give the answer to them all, so far as it is His will that we should understand them down here. There will always be mysteries beyond our understanding, for God's ways are not our ways, and His thoughts are not our thoughts (Isaiah 55:8).

But the trusting soul learns to be content with what He has revealed, and so to quietly leave the rest to be unfolded in that coming day when we will see Him as He is, and in His light will see light, and know even as we ourselves are known of Him (1 Corinthians 13:12).

Someone was once asked, "How do you know that Jesus lives – that He has actually been raised from the dead?"

"Why," was the answer, "I have just come from a half-hour's talk with Him. I know I cannot be mistaken."

And this testimony might be multiplied by millions who, through all the Christian centuries, have borne witness to the reality of the personal companionship of Christ Jesus by the Spirit, drawing out the heart in love and devotion, and answering prayer in such a way as to make it impossible to doubt His tender care.

The late Robert T. Grant told me that on one occasion, while travelling, he was sitting in the Pullman reading his Bible. He noticed the people around, many with nothing to do. He opened up his bag and got out some gospel tracts, and after distributing them he sat down again.

A young man left his own seat and moved over to the preacher, and asked, "What did you give this to me for?"

"Why, it is a message from heaven for you, to give you rest in your soul," replied Mr. Grant.

The young man sneered and said, "I used to believe in that stuff years ago, but when I went to school and got educated, I threw it all overboard. I found out there's nothing to it."

"Will you let me read to you something I was going over just a moment ago?" Mr. Grant said. "'The Lord is my shepherd: I shall not want.' (Psalm 23 KJV) Is there nothing in that, young man? I have known the blessedness of that for many years. Is there nothing in it?"

The young man replied, "Go on, read what comes next."

"'He maketh me to lie down in green pastures: he leadeth me beside the still waters. He restoreth my soul: he leadeth me in the paths of righteousness for his name's sake.' Is there nothing in that?"

"Pardon me, sir, let me hear some more," said the

young man.

"'Yea, though I walk through the valley of the shadow of death, I will fear no evil: for thou art with me; thy rod and thy staff they comfort me.' Is there nothing in that?"

Then the young man cried, "Oh, forgive me, sir, there is everything in that! My mother died with those words on her lips and besought me to trust her Savior, but I have gotten far away from Him. You have brought it all back. Tell me more."

As God's servant opened up the truth as to the way of salvation, the young man who had been so careless and unbelieving was convicted of his sin, and led to trust in Jesus and confess Him as His own Savior right there in that Pullman car.

Yes, there is everything in the blessed companionship of Jesus Christ, the Lord, both in life and in death, and it is this that gives the full assurance of hope.

But, unhappily, this assurance can become clouded, and in a measure lost by spiritual negligence and carelessness in regard to prayer and feeding on the Word. Therefore the need of such an exhortation as we have before us, which urges us to *show the same diligence so as to realize the full assurance of hope until the end*" (Hebrews 6:11).

Peter speaks of some who through waywardness have gotten so far out of fellowship with God that they have forgotten their purification from their former sins (2 Peter 1:9).This is a sad state to be in. It is what is commonly called in the Old Testament "backsliding." And "*the backslider in heart will have his fill of his own ways, but a good man will be satisfied with his*" (Proverbs14:14). An old preacher I knew as a boy used to say, "Backsliding always begins in the knee." And this is very true indeed.

Neglect of prayer will soon dull the keen edge of one's spiritual sensibilities, and make it easy for a believer to drift into worldliness and selfish pleasures. As a result of this, their soul's eyesight will become dimmed and they will lose the heavenly vision.

It is not merely that we are now saved by grace, but we are also in the school of grace. We are here to learn how to behave ourselves in such a manner as to have the constant approval of Him who has made us His own.

And so grace is here presented as our instructor, teaching us the importance of the denial of self, and the refusal of all that is contrary to the mind of God, in order that we can show by clean and holy lives the reality of the faith that we profess. All the while, we always have before our souls that blessed certainty of the appearing of the glory of our great God and Savior Jesus Christ.

At His first coming, Jesus died to redeem us from all lawlessness, that He might purify us to Himself a people of His own possession, zealously engaged in all good works (Titus 2:14). At His second coming He will redeem our bodies and make us wholly like Himself in all things (Philippians 3:21). What a wonderful thought this is. And as we live in the power of it, what assurance we have of the unchanging love of Him whose face we soon will see!

Often when the dead in Christ are being laid away, we are reminded that we commit their precious bodies to the grave "*in the sure and certain hope of a glorious resurrection.*"

And this is a most blessed truth. For when the hope of the Lord's return is realized, the saints of all past ages who died in faith will share with those who can be alive on the earth at that time, in the wonderful change that will then take place when "*the Lord Himself will descend from heaven with a shout, with the voice of the archangel and with the trumpet of God, and the dead in Christ will rise first. Then we who are alive and remain will be caught up together with them in the clouds to meet the Lord in the air, and so we shall always be with the Lord*" (1 Thessalonians 4:16-17).

How bright a promise is this, and who knows how soon it may be realized! Let us not falter, or give way to doubt or unbelief, but give diligence in maintaining "*the full assurance of hope*" until it gives place to full realization.

Meantime, let us be busy in our Master's service, and particularly in trying to win others, bringing them to share with us in the joy of God's salvation. When at last our little day of service here is ended, not one of us will feel that we have given up too much for Jesus Christ, or be sorry that we have labored too earnestly for His glory.

But I fear many of us would then give worlds, were they ours, if we could only go back to earth and live our lives over again, in sincerity and unselfishness, seeking alone the honor of Him who has redeemed us.

It is better to be saved so as by fire (1 Corinthians 3:12-15), than not to be saved at all. But surely none of us would desire to meet our Master empty-handed, but would rather be "*coming with shouts of joy*" into His presence, when our hope is fulfilled, bringing our sheaves with us (Psalm 126:6).

Chapter 5

Jesus is Alive!

The basic ground for this assurance, not only of the individual salvation of each believer, but of the eventual carrying out of the divine program in its entirety, rests solely on the resurrection of our Lord Jesus Christ. This is emphasized by the apostle Paul in his great sermon addressed to the Athenian philosophers on Mars Hill, as recorded in Acts 17.

There, after pointing out the unreasonableness and wicked folly of idolatry, Paul declared the truth as to the Unknown God, the Creator of heaven and earth. Then he added: *"Therefore having overlooked the times of ignorance, God is now declaring to men that all people everywhere should repent, because He has fixed a day in which He will judge the world in righteousness through a Man whom He has appointed, having furnished proof to all men by raising Him from the dead"* (Acts 17:30-31).

Paul had himself received visual proof of that resurrection of which he spoke. The risen Jesus had appeared to him as he fell to the ground on the Damascus road, overcome by a supernatural light from heaven.

At this very time there were many living witnesses of the greatest miracle of all the ages, for when writing to the Corinthian church, some years later than his visit to Athens, Paul enumerated considerably over five hundred who could bear positive testimony to the resurrection of our Lord.

"He appeared to Cephas, then to the twelve. After that He appeared to more than five hundred brethren at one time, most of whom remain until now, but some have fallen asleep" (1 Corinthians 15:5-6).

Horace Bushnell declared that the resurrection of Jesus Christ is the best attested fact of ancient history. Think of the authoritative sources for any other outstanding event, and compare them with the proofs of the resurrection, and you will realize the fairness of this remark.

The writers of the four Gospels were men of the sincerest godliness and honesty, as their works show. They unite in giving unqualified testimony to the resurrection of Jesus. The other New Testament writers, Paul, James, Peter, and Jude definitely mention or clearly imply the same glorious fact. They all speak of Jesus as the living One, who once died for our sins. Concerning what other ancient historical event can the testimony of so many eyewitnesses be cited?

Even the enemies of the gospel bore unwilling witness to the resurrection by their clumsy efforts to interpret to their advantage the empty grave on that first Easter Sunday. They knew Jesus had predicted that He would rise again in three days, and so they went to Pilate demanding that steps be taken to prevent His disciples from stealing the body of their Master.

Pilate gave them a guard and commanded the sealing of the tomb, and grimly added, *"Make it as secure as you know how!"* (Matthew 27:65). But all their efforts were in vain. When the appointed hour struck, angelic hands broke the Roman imperial seal and rolled back the stone, revealing an empty grave – the body was not there.

Certainly none of His foes rifled that grave. They were determined to keep the body of Jesus there as long as time should last. If they could have produced that body later, in order to disprove the message of the resurrection, certainly they would have done so.

And it is preposterous to credit the story circulated by the wily priesthood that Jesus' disciples came by night and stole away His body. *"For as yet they did not understand the Scripture, that He must rise again from the dead"* (John 20:9). The amazing thing is that His enemies remembered what His friends had forgotten. The empty tomb was as great a shock to those who loved Jesus, as it was a fearful portent to those who hated Him.

Only the personal appearances of the risen Jesus, with all the marks of His crucifixion, convinced them of the reality of His resurrection. The following forty days during which He appeared to them on many occasions, instructing them concerning the Kingdom of God, furnished ample proof that He had really triumphed over death.

This glorious fact gave them that confidence which enabled them to stand against all opposition, witnessing to everyone that God had raised Jesus' body from the grave.

They watched as He was taken up from them into heaven in that same body, and after receiving the Pentecostal power to be witnesses, power for mission, they went about bearing witness to the resurrection of their Lord.

This is the outstanding message of the Church. He

who died for our sins lives again for our justification. The resurrection of the material body of flesh and bones is the proof that God is satisfied with the redemptive work of His Son. It declares that God can now be just, and the justifier of those who believe in the Lord Jesus. To say that though Christ is *dead* as to the body, He is alive as to the spirit will not do. That might be true of any man. It would be no evidence of divine satisfaction in His work.

Some years ago an eloquent New York preacher, who denied the physical resurrection of the Savior, declared, "The body of Jesus still sleeps in an unknown Syrian tomb, but His soul goes marching on!"

Many applauded this as a wonderful explanation of the influence of Jesus down through the ages. But it is utterly false. If the body of Jesus still rests in the grave, He was not Who He professed to be – and is powerless to save.

This heresy (for heresy it is) is not new. It became prevalent in certain circles even in apostolic days, as 1 Corinthians 15 proves. In the Corinthian church there were some who accepted the teaching of the Sadducees and denied the reality of a literal resurrection.

Sternly, Paul challenges them in the well-known words: *"Now if Christ is preached, that He has been raised from the dead, how do some among you say that there is no resurrection of the dead? But if there is no resurrection of the dead, not even Christ has been raised; and if Christ has not been raised, then our preaching is vain, your faith also is vain. Moreover we are even found to be false witnesses of God, because we testified against God that He raised Christ, whom He did not raise, if in fact the dead are not raised. For if the dead are not raised, not even Christ has been raised; and if Christ has not been raised, your faith is worthless*" (1 Corinthians 15:12-19).

Here is sturdy logic indeed, inspired by the Holy Spirit. If Jesus has not risen we have no gospel to preach, and there is no message of deliverance for poor, lost sinners held captive in chains of iniquity. Faith in a dead Jesus will not save anyone. The gospel is the power of God to salvation, because it proclaims a living, loving Redeemer who is waiting to make His power known on behalf of all who trust in Him.

Let us then notice carefully what the Word of God tells us about this glorious truth.

First: The resurrection of the Lord Jesus attests the truthfulness of His claims concerning His divine person and mission. To His enemies He said, "*Destroy this temple, and in three days I will raise it up*" (John 2:19). But He spoke of the temple of His body.

To His disciples Jesus declared, "*No one has taken it away from Me, but I lay it down on My own initiative. I have authority to lay it down, and I have authority to take it up again. This commandment I received from My Father*" (John 10:18).

Jesus definitely told them that the Son of man must be betrayed into the hands of sinners, and He added, "*After they have scourged Him, they will kill Him; and the third day He will rise again.*" (Luke 18:33).

Therefore if Jesus failed to come out of the tomb in a resurrected, physical body of flesh and bones, all that He claimed regarding Himself and His saving power was invalidated. But He did not fail! It was not possible that He could be held captive by death. He fulfilled His Word by rising again on the third day.

Second: Jesus' resurrection attests the truth of the prophetic Scriptures. The Old Testament is full of prophecies of Messiah's death and resurrection. In Psalm 16:10, David foretold concerning Him, "*For You will not abandon my soul to Sheol* (the place of the dead)*; nor will You allow Your Holy One to undergo decay.*" Both Peter and Paul show us that this passage had its fulfillment in the resurrection of Jesus.

Isaiah wrote seven hundred years before Jesus' birth, "*But the Lord was pleased to crush Him, putting Him to grief; if He would render Himself as a guilt offering, He will see His offspring, He will prolong His days, and the good pleasure of the Lord will prosper in His hand*" (Isaiah 53:10).

Here is a remarkable statement. Death was not to end the activities of Jehovah's Servant. After He had given His life as a full offering for sin, He was to prolong His days, and so in resurrection be the Administrator of God's great plan for the blessing of mankind.

Third: The resurrection of the Lord Jesus was the display of omnipotent power on our behalf. In Ephesians 1:17-23 we have the apostle Paul's prayer for all believers. He asks that the eyes of their hearts might be opened, in order that they might know the hope of His calling; the riches of the glory of His inheritance in the saints; and "*the surpassing greatness of His power toward us who believe. These are in accordance with the working of the strength of His might which He brought about in Christ, when He raised Him from the dead.*"

The same mighty energy that was used to bring the body of Jesus back to life from among the dead, is the power that quickens dead souls into newness of life. It

43

energizes children of God so as to enable them to live a heavenly life of victory over sin even here on earth, while they walk in fellowship with Him under the control of His Holy Spirit.

Fourth: The resurrection of Jesus is the proof that the sin question has been settled to God's satisfaction. On the cross our sins were laid on Him. He voluntarily accepted responsibility for them. He bore them in His own body on the cross. *"He who was delivered over because of our transgressions, and was raised because of our justification"* (Romans 4:25).

When God raised His Son from death it was His way of expressing His recognition of the perfection of His finished work. If sin had not been put away for ever, Jesus would never have come out from that grave. But having paid for us the uttermost farthing, death had no claim on Him. By raising Him, God declared to all created intelligences His full approval of, and His acceptance of, the work of His blessed Son.

Fifth: Jesus' resurrection is therefore the believing sinner's assurance that their record is now clear. God Himself has no charge against anyone who puts their trust in Jesus. So we read in Romans 8:32-34: *"He who did not spare His own Son, but delivered Him over for us all, how will He not also with Him freely give us all things? Who will bring a charge against God's elect? God is the one who justifies; who is the one who condemns? Christ Jesus is He who died, yes, rather who was raised, who is at the right hand of God, who also intercedes for us."*

Observe that no voice can now be raised to condemn *anyone* who rests in Jesus Christ's finished work. His death and resurrection forbid the raising of the sin question again, as far as any believer is concerned. The resurrection is like a receipt for full payment made. On the cross the mighty debt we owed was settled. A risen Jesus tells us that every claim has been met – and God holds *nothing* against the believer.

Sixth: Jesus' resurrection is the way that through Him God will judge the world. That judgment is based on man's attitude toward the One who the Father delights to honor. If we receive Him as Lord and Savior we will never have to come into judgment for our sins – because He was judged in our place. But if we refuse Him and spurn His grace, we will not only have to answer before Him for all our sins, but in addition to all the rest, we will be judged for rejecting Him who died to save us.

Lastly: It is Jesus' resurrection which alone gives validity to the gospel message, and delivers the believer from the fear of death.

Turning now to 2 Timothy 1:8-10, we read this important warning from Paul: *"Therefore do not be ashamed of the testimony of our Lord or of me His prisoner, but join with me in suffering for the gospel according to the power of God, who has saved us and called us with a holy calling, not according to our works, but according to His own purpose and grace which was granted us in Christ Jesus from all eternity, but now has been revealed by the appearing of our Savior Christ Jesus, who abolished death and brought life and immortality to light through the gospel."*

Do not, I beg you, read these words hastily. Go over them again and again, until their force and their solemnity and their preciousness have gripped your soul. Our entire salvation hangs on the truth that our

Savior, Jesus Christ, has abolished (that is, annulled the power of) death, and has brought life and immortality to light through the gospel.

Jesus went down into the dark stream of death. All its waves and billows rolled over Him, but He came up in resurrection life – never to die again. And so for us the waters of this Jordan have been rolled back, and there is a dry way through death for all who believe.

Listen to Jesus' triumphant words. *"I am the resurrection and the life; he who believes in Me will live even if he dies, and everyone who lives and believes in Me will never die. Do you believe this?"* (John 11:25-26.)

Does not your heart reply, "Yes, Lord, I do believe. I rest my soul forevermore on Your sure testimony, and I confess You as my Savior and my Lord"?

It is thus that God gives assurance to everyone that He has raised Jesus from the dead. If Satan tries to discourage you by occupying you with your own unworthiness and your many shortcomings, do not attempt to argue with him, but look up to the throne of God – and there contemplate the risen One who once hung a bleeding Victim on the cross of shame, and whose lifeless body once lay in Joseph's new tomb. Remember, He could not be yonder in the glory if one sin remained unsettled. Therefore, every believer can sing with assurance:

> "The Lord is risen, with Him we also rose,
> And in His death see vanquished all our foes.
> The Lord is risen, we stand beyond the doom
> Of all our sins, through Jesus' empty tomb."

The young convert was right, who said, when this truth was revealed to him by the Spirit: "If anyone is ever to be kept out of heaven for my sins, it will have to be Jesus, for He took them all upon Himself and made Himself responsible for them. But He is in heaven already, never to be turned out, so now I know that I am secure as long as He lives, the One who once died in my place."

This expresses it exactly, for faith is just saying "Amen" to what God has made known in His Word. The believer sets to his seal that God is true, and so rests everything for eternity on the fact that Jesus, who died for our sins on the cross of shame, has been raised to endless life.

It is noticeable that the entire Trinity of the God-head are concerned in this marvelous event, and each divine Person participated in our Lord's rising from among the dead.

As we have already seen, His resurrection is attributed to Himself: "*No one has taken it away from Me, but I lay it down on My own initiative. I have authority to lay it down, and I have authority to take it up again. This commandment I received from My Father*" (John 10:18). Again, Jesus said, "*Destroy this temple, and in three days I will raise it up*" (John 2:19).

It is also attributed to the Father: "*Now the God of peace, who brought up from the dead the great Shepherd of the sheep through the blood of the eternal covenant, even Jesus our Lord*" (Hebrews 13:20).

The Holy Spirit is likewise recognized as the direct Agent in bringing to pass this stupendous miracle: "*But if the Spirit of Him who raised Jesus from the dead dwells in you, He who raised Christ Jesus from the dead will also give life to your mortal bodies through His Spirit who dwells in you"* (Romans 8:11).

And so each Person of the Godhead is concerned in proclaiming the testimony of Jesus and His resurrection to men and women everywhere – those who are dead in trespasses and sins, until quickened by the same mighty power that raised up our blessed Lord and set Him at God's right hand in the highest heaven.

There is a very precious line of truth unfolded in John's First Epistle that has to do with some of the basics of Christian living. In 1 John 3:18-19 we are both exhorted and encouraged in the following words: *"Little children, let us not love with word or with tongue, but in deed and truth. We will know by this that we are of the truth, and will assure our heart before Him."*

Now this assurance of heart is the result of the Spirit's work in the believer, following the full assurance of faith. The moment I take God at His Word and trust the Lord Jesus as my Savior, I have eternal life. I know it on the authority of the Holy Scriptures, which over and over link the present possession of this life with faith in the One who God gave to be the sacrifice for our sins.

As I go on in the Christian life I have abundant corroborative evidence through the Holy Spirit's continuous work in my inmost being that this is indeed far more than a doctrine which I have accepted.

I find from day to day positive proofs that I am in very truth a new person, *"For we are His workmanship, created in Christ Jesus for good works, which God prepared beforehand so that we would walk in them"* (Ephesians 2:10). Thus my assurance deepens.

While at the beginning I rested everything for eternity on the naked Word of God, I find, as I continue in faith, overwhelming confirmation of the truth of that Word in the manifestations of eternal life actually imparted to me a sinner, through grace.

The believer becomes conscious of an inborn love for the will of God. *"By this we know that we have come to know Him, if we keep His commandments. The one who says, 'I have come to know Him,' and does not keep His commandments, is a liar, and the truth is not in him; but whoever keeps His word, in him the love of God has truly been perfected. By this we know that we are in Him"* (1 John 2:3-5).

It is not natural for the *un*believer to delight in the will of God. The unsaved person loves their own way and resents being asked to yield their will to another. If we come to Jesus in repentance, we can sing:

> Blessed assurance, Jesus is mine!
> Oh, what a foretaste of glory divine!
> Heir of salvation, purchase of God,
> born of his Spirit, washed in his blood.

PART TWO

Difficulties Which Hinder Full Assurance

It is now my aim to consider some of the difficulties and perplexities which keep souls from entering into peace, and enjoying the full assurance of salvation. These questions and objections are some that have come to me again and again from earnest seekers after light, and are therefore, I have good reason to believe, fairly representative of the troublesome thoughts that hinder many from seeing the simplicity of God's way of life, as set out in His holy Word. Perhaps if you do not have a settled rest of heart and conscience, you will find your own particular troubles dealt with here.

1. *"How can I be sure that I have repented enough?"*
Very often the real difficulty arises from a misapprehension of the meaning of repentance. There is no salvation without repentance, but it is important to see exactly what is meant by this term. It should not be confused with penitence, which is sorrow for sin; nor with penance, which is an effort to make some sort of amends for sin; nor yet with reformation, which is turning from sin.

Repentance is a change of attitude toward sin, toward self, and toward God. The original word (in the Greek Testament) literally means "a change of mind."

This is not a mere intellectual change of viewpoint, however, but a complete reversal of attitude.

Now test yourself in this way. You once lived in sin and loved it. Do you now desire deliverance from it? You were once self-confident and trusting in your own fancied goodness. Do you now judge yourself as a sinner before God? You once sought to hide from God and rebelled against His authority. Do you now look up to Him, desiring to know Him, and to yield yourself to Him? If you can honestly say "Yes" to these questions, you have repented. Your attitude is altogether different to what it once was.

You confess you are a sinner, unable to cleanse your own soul, and you are willing to be saved in God's way. This is repentance. And remember, it is not the *amount* of repentance that counts: it is the fact that you turn from self to God that puts you in the place where His grace avails through Jesus Christ.

Strictly speaking, not one of us has ever repented enough. None of us has realized the enormity of our guilt as God sees it. But when we judge ourselves and trust the Savior He has provided, we are saved through His merits. As recipients of His lovingkindness, repentance will be deepened and will continue day by day, as we learn more and more of His infinite worth and our own unworthiness.

2. *"I don't feel fit for God. I'm so unworthy, I fear He won't take me in."*

What a wretched condition would be yours if you imagined you were good enough, in yourself, for heaven – or that you were worthy of such love as God has shown! It is because of your *lack* of merit that Jesus died to redeem you. It is because you are worthy only of eternal judgment that God *"made Him, who knew no sin to be sin on our behalf, so that we might become the righteousness of God in Him"* (2 Corinthians 5:21). If you had any merit of your own, you would not need a Savior.

When the Roman centurion sought the healing power of Jesus for his servant, he sent the Jewish elders to the Lord to intercede for him. In Luke chapter 7 we read that the people told Jesus, *"He is worthy for You to grant this to him; for he loves our nation and it was he who built us our synagogue."* But the centurion sent a message to Jesus, *"I am not worthy for You to come under my roof."*

They said, *"He is worthy"*; he declared, *"I am not worthy,"* and this moved the heart of Jesus, so that He exclaimed, *"Not even in Israel have I found such great faith."*

So long as someone considers themselves worthy, there is no salvation for them; but when, in repentance, they admit their unworthiness, there is immediate deliverance for them through faith in the Lord Jesus Christ. Without repentance, the sinner is unable to believe to salvation.

3. *"I'm afraid I'm too great a sinner to ever be saved!'*

But Jesus did not come to call the *righteous*, but *sinners* to repentance. He did not die for good people, and in truth there are no basically good people in the world. *"All have turned aside, together they have become useless; there is none who does good, there is not even one"* (Romans 3:12). But if anyone imagines they are good in themselves, there is no salvation for them. *"But when Jesus heard this, He said, 'It is not those who are healthy who need a physician, but those who are sick'"* (Matthew 9:12).

Sin is like a deadly disease that fastens on the whole being, but Jesus is the great Physician who cures the worst of cases. No one can be too vile, or too sinful, or too wicked for Him. His skill is unlimited. He delights to show great grace to great sinners. The apostle Paul said, *"It is a trustworthy statement, deserving full acceptance, that Christ Jesus came into the world to save sinners, among whom I am foremost of all* (1 Timothy 1:15), but he was saved in that moment when he trusted the Lord Jesus.

The greater your sinfulness, the more you need the Savior. And the worse your condition, the more proof you have that you are the one for whom He died. God laid all our sins upon His Son when He hung on that cross of Calvary. He suffered for them *all*. Not *one* of your sins was overlooked.

There is such infinite value in Jesus' death on the cross, that grace can now be extended to the vilest sinner on the face of the earth – if they will only receive the Lord Jesus by faith as their personal Savior.

4. *"But what if I'm not one of the elect?"*

You can readily settle that yourself. Without attempting to delve into the mysteries of the divine decrees and the divine foreknowledge, it is enough to say that all who come to God through His Son are elect. Jesus makes this very plain in John 6:37. He says, *"All that the Father gives Me will come to Me, and the one who comes to Me I will certainly not cast out."*

Now do not linger too long on the first half of the

verse. Be clear about the latter half, for it is there that *your* responsibility is found. Have you come to Jesus? If so, you have His pledged word that He will not cast you out. The fact that you come, proves that the Father gave you to Jesus. Thus you can be certain that you belong to the glorious company of the elect.

D. L. Moody used to put it very simply: "The elect are the 'whosoever wills'; the non-elect are the 'whosoever won'ts.'" This is exactly what Scripture teaches. The invitation is to all. Remember, we are never told that Jesus died for the elect. But what does the Word say? "*Christ died for the ungodly*" (Romans 5:6). Are you ungodly? Then He died for you! Put in your claim and enter into peace.

Meditate on the Holy Spirit's declaration through the apostle Paul: "*It is a trustworthy statement, deserving full acceptance, that Christ Jesus came into the world to save sinners*" Nowhere are we told that Christ came to save the elect.

The term "sinners" is all-embracing, "*for all have sinned and fall short of the glory of God*" (Romans 3:23). Are you *sure* you are a sinner? You are? Then you can be *certain* there is salvation for you. Do not concern yourself in matters too high for you. Just be simple enough to take God at His word.

5. "*Sometimes I'm afraid that I'm predestinated to be damned. If so, I can do nothing to alter my terrible case.*"

No one was ever predestinated to be damned. Predestination is a precious truth of inestimable value and comfort, when rightly understood. Turn to your Bible and read for yourself in the only two chapters in which this word "predestinate" or "predestinated" relating to people is found?

The first is Romans 8:29-30: "*For those whom He foreknew, He also predestined to become conformed to the image of His Son, so that He would be the firstborn among many brethren; and these whom He predestined, He also called; and these whom He called, He also justified; and these whom He justified, He also glorified.*"

The other chapter is Ephesians 1. In verse 5 we read: "*He predestined us to adoption as sons through Jesus Christ to Himself, according to the kind intention of His will.*" And in verse 11, it says: "*also we have obtained an inheritance, having been predestined according to His purpose who works all things after the counsel of His will.*"

You will note that there is no reference in these verses to either heaven or hell, but to Christlikeness eventually. Nowhere are we told in Scripture that God predestinated one person to be saved and another to be lost. We are to be saved or lost eternally because of our attitude toward the Lord Jesus Christ. "*He who believes in the Son has eternal life; but he who does not obey the Son will not see life, but the wrath of God abides on him*" (John 3:36).

Predestination means that some day all the redeemed will become just like the Lord Jesus! Is not this precious? Do not try to make a bugaboo out of that which was intended to give joy and comfort to those who trust in the Savior. Trust Him for yourself, and you will know that God has predestinated you to be fully conformed to the image of His Son.

6. *"I'm trying to believe, but I have no assurance of salvation."*

Who are you trying to believe? Would you dare speak of *trying* to believe God who cannot lie? Is not this to insult God to His face? Suppose a close friend of yours related a strange story which they declared to be a fact, would you say, "I will *try* to believe you."? Would not this be tantamount to declaring that you did not believe them at all? Do not then, I beg of you, talk of *trying* to believe, when God has given His own testimony concerning His Son, and promised to give eternal life to *all* who trust Him.

You either do believe God, or you do not. If you do not believe Him, you are in effect calling Him a liar. If you have been doing this up to now, will you not go to Him at once and confess this great wickedness of which you have been guilty, and tell Him you will now rest in simple faith on His word? It is not a question of *feeling* or *emotion*, but of *"believing* God and asking no questions," as that little boy put it, when asked "What is faith?"

7. *"But shouldn't I feel different?"*

There is nothing in Scripture to say that our eternal safety depends on our *feelings*. Take Paul's sermon to the Athenians, which has caused some confusion about the place of feelings. He rebukes them for imagining the Godhead to be like silver and gold, and shows that the true God is the Creator of all things:

"He made from one man every nation of mankind to live on all the face of the earth, having determined their appointed times and the boundaries of their habitation, that they would seek God, if perhaps they

might **grope** *for Him and find Him, though He is not far from each one of us*" (Acts 17:26-27).

Although some Bible translations have the word "feel" right in the center of this passage, it has nothing to do with the gospel, but rather with the unbeliever groping in the dark. You are not in their situation. You have heard the gospel. You know of the one living and true God. You are not told to *feel* anything, but to *believe* His record.

Ignore your feelings altogether, and tell the Lord Jesus now that you will trust Him and confess Him before others.

8. *"I can see that God has done His part in the work of my salvation, but don't I have to do my part if I would benefit with what He has done?"*

Have you ever heard the story of the man who was wonderfully saved and arose in a class meeting to testify to his new-found joy? His heart was filled with Jesus, and his lips spoke of Him and of Him only, as his Redeemer and Lord.

The class leader was a legalist, and said when the other had finished, "Our brother has told us what the Lord did for him, but he has forgotten to tell us what *he* did in order to be saved. God does His part when we do ours. Brother, did you not do your part before God saved you?"

The man was on his feet in a moment, and exclaimed, "I sure did do my part. I took to running away from God as fast as my sins could carry me. That was *my* part. And God took after me till He ran me down. That was *His* part."

Yes, you and I have all done our part, and a dreadfully sad part it was. We did all the *sinning*, and He must do all the *saving*. Then, *after* we are saved, we can labor night and day to show our gratitude to Him for what His grace has wrought.

9. *"It is not exactly that I don't trust God, but I can't be sure of myself. I'm even afraid my faith is unreal."*

Faith is not the Savior – Jesus is. He is the unchanging One. *"Jesus Christ is the same yesterday and today and forever"* (Hebrews 13:8). Faith is just the hand that lays hold of Him. You are not asked to trust yourself. The less confidence you have in yourself the better. Put all your confidence in the Lord Jesus. He is not unreal, and if your faith is centered in Him all will be well for time and eternity.

10. *"But the Bible says faith is the gift of God, and that all men don't have faith. Perhaps it's not the will of God to give me saving faith."*

Faith is the gift of God in this sense, that only through His Word is it received. *"So faith comes from hearing, and hearing by the word of Christ"* (Romans 10:17). Everyone can have faith if they will; but alas, many refuse to hear the Word of God,

11. *"What troubles me is that I'm not sure I have accepted Jesus."*

To accept Jesus is to receive Him by faith as your Lord and Savior. But, strictly speaking, the great thing to see is that God has accepted Him. Jesus took our sins and died to make full payment for them – and God has raised Him from the dead and taken Him up to glory.

God has accepted Jesus in token of His perfect satisfaction in His work. Believing this, the soul enters into peace. I simply rest in God's thoughts about His Son.

12. *"Sometimes I believe I've trusted Jesus and I'm justified before God, but I can't forget my sins. They come before me night and day. Surely, if I were really forgiven I could forget the past."*

Ah, dear troubled one, the closer you get to Jesus, and the more deeply you repent of your sins, the more you will hate yourself for ever committing them. But let your comfort be in this blessed thought – *God* has forgotten them! He says, *"For I will be merciful to their iniquities, and I will remember their sins no more"* (Hebrews 8:12).

So when your sins come into your mind to trouble and distress you, just rest in the fact that God has forgotten them, and will never bring them up again. Jesus has settled for all of those sins. Believe it, and be at peace.

13. *"I often come to the point of deciding for Jesus, then I draw back because I'm afraid I won't be able to hold out!"*

If it were a matter of your own ability to hold out, you might well fear. You have no power in yourself that will enable you to hold out. But the moment you fully trust the Lord Jesus, you are born again. Then the Holy Spirit comes to dwell in your heart to be the power of the new life. He will enable you to resist temptation and to live to the glory of God.

"For it is God who is at work in you, both to will and to work for His good pleasure" (Philippians 2:13). Do not count on self at all. Let Him have His way. He

will lead you on in triumph as you surrender to Him.

14. *"But must I not hold on to the end if I would be saved at the last?"*

May I, without irreverence, venture to recast a Bible story? If the account of Noah and the flood went something like this, what would you think of it? Suppose that after the ark was completed, God said to Noah, "Now, get eight great spikes and drive them into the side of the ark."

So Noah procured the spikes and did as he was told. Then God said to him, "Now, everyone in your house must hang onto these spikes." And Noah and his wife, and the three sons and their wives, each caught hold of a spike. And the rains descended and the flood came, and as the ark was borne up on the waters their muscles were strained to the utmost as they clung to the spikes.

Imagine God then saying to them, "If you hang on till the deluge is over, you will be saved!" Can you even think of such a thing as any one of them going safely through?

But oh, how different the simple Bible story. *"Then the Lord said to Noah, 'Enter the ark, you and all your household'"* (Genesis 7:1). Ah, that is a very different thing to holding on! Inside the ark they were safe while the ark endured the storm. And every believer is in Jesus Christ, and is perfectly safe. Look away then from all self-effort, and trust Him alone. Rest in the Ark, and rejoice in God's great salvation.

Be sure to remember that it is *Jesus* who holds *you*, not you who hold *Him*. He has said, *"I will never desert you, nor will I ever forsake you"* (Hebrews 13:5). *"For if while we were enemies we were reconciled to God through the death of His Son, much more, having been reconciled, we shall be saved by His life"* (Romans 5:10).

He who died for you, now lives at God's right hand to keep you – and the Father sees you in Him, *"to the praise of the glory of His grace, which He freely bestowed on us in the Beloved"* (Ephesians 1:6). Could anything be more sure?

15. *"Don't I have to strive if I would enter in at the narrow door? It seems to me just believing is too easy a way!"* (See Luke 13:24, where Jesus says, *"Strive to enter through the narrow door; for many, I tell you, will seek to enter and will not be able."*)

Our Lord's words may well give us pause. They were never intended, however, to make us feel that a hard struggle was necessary in order to be saved. But Jesus would have us understand that no one will ever be saved who is not in earnest.

The great majority of people drift aimlessly and carelessly on, passing heedlessly by the door/gate to life, intent only on gratifying their worldly desires. The person who would be saved must arouse themselves to the supreme importance of spiritual things. They must put first things first. In this sense they strive to enter in at the narrow gate.

The seeker will be like Bunyan's Pilgrim who, when awakened to his danger and realizing the dreadful burden of sin, refused to heed the pleadings of his old companions, and putting his fingers in his ears, cried, "Life, life, eternal life!" as he fled from the City of Destruction. You, too, must determine that nothing will be allowed to interfere with the settlement of the great matter of the salvation of your soul.

But do you have to strive with God to save you? No, He is waiting to do that very thing for you. Yes, and He will do it for you the moment you cease from all self-effort and put your trust in Jesus.

To strive to enter in is to be determined that nothing will keep you from accepting the gracious invitation of the Lord Jesus, who bids you come to Him in all your need and guilt, that He will fit you for heaven's glory by cleansing you from every stain. Do not on any account be turned away from this, but brushing every barrier aside, yield your heart to the Savior now.

16. *"Don't I have to wait for God's time? I can do nothing about it until He's ready to save me."*

But God's time is *now*. He plainly tells us, *"Come to Me, all who are weary and heavy-laden, and I will give you rest"* (Matthew 11:28). You need not wait another moment. He will never be any more ready to save you than He is at the very instant you are reading these words – and you will never be more fit to come to Him than at this very moment. Just as you are.

Every day you wait you are adding to the terrible list of your sins. Every hour you continue to reject Him you are increasing your guilt by refusing to receive His blessed Son.

Every moment you stay away from Him you are sinning against His love. Why not close up the present evil record by coming to Him now and, owning your need, accept the gift of God which is eternal life?

17. *"I really want to come to Jesus, but I don't seem to know how to do it."*

It is strange how we stumble over the very simplicity of the gospel invitation. Jesus is a living, loving, divinely-human personality – as truly as when He was here on earth. It is He Himself who bids us come.

Do you know what it is to stay away? Then surely you need have no difficulty in doing the very opposite! Lift your heart to Him in prayer. Tell Him that you are the sinner for whom He died, and that now you accept His gracious invitation to *"Come; for everything is ready now"* (Luke 14:17). Then believe that He receives you, for He said He would, and He always keeps His word.

You may have heard the story of Charlotte Elliot, the hymn writer. As a young woman she was troubled and anxious about her soul, but very reticent when it came to seeking help from others. But a French pastor, who was visiting her father, put the question directly to her during a meal, "Have you come to Jesus?"

She replied, "I want to come, but I do not know how."

He simply answered, "Come just as you are."

She fled to her room in tears and later emerged a saved soul. She wrote the well-known lines quoted below as the expression of her own coming. If you have not already done so, will you not make them yours?

"Just as I am, without one plea,
But that Thy blood was shed for me,
And that Thou bidd'st me come to Thee,
O Lamb of God! I come!

"Just as I am, Thy love unknown
Hath broken ev'ry barrier down;

Now to be Thine, yea, Thine alone,
O Lamb of God, I come!"

18. *"Don't I have to pray through until I get the testimony, the witness, that I am saved?"*

Nowhere in the Bible are people told they must keep praying to be saved. It is true that the natural expression of an awakened and anxious soul is prayer. But there is no such thing in Scripture as "praying through" in order to be saved. What is required is that the convicted sinner believes the gospel – literally the Good News.

Suppose a man went home tired and hungry, and said to his wife, "Will you please let me have supper as early as possible?" She complies at once and sets the table, calling him to come and partake of what she has provided. Instead of doing so, he pleads long and earnestly, literally begging for food. What would she think of him?

And what does God think when He has spread the gospel feast for starving sinners and invited all to "come and dine," but instead of obeying His voice, people fall on their knees and beg and plead for His mercy and grace, and do not accept His invitation and feast on the Living Bread provided for their salvation.

The witness of the Spirit is only enjoyed by those who thus take Him at His Word. The believer has received the testimony as given in the Word of God. *"And the Holy Spirit also testifies to us"* (Hebrews 10:15). The believers have the testimony in themselves because the truth has been received into their heart.

"The one who believes in the Son of God has the testimony in himself; the one who does not believe God

has made Him a liar, because he has not believed in the testimony that God has given concerning His Son" (1 John 5:10). We enjoy the Spirit's witnessing with our spirit when, upon believing, the Holy Spirit comes to dwell within. "*The Spirit Himself testifies with our spirit that we are children of God*" (Romans 8:16).

This is not a happy feeling. It is the *testimony* that the Spirit gives through the Word. That this testimony brings joy and gladness goes without question. I do not *know* I am saved simply *because* I feel happy. But I *feel* happy *because* I know I am saved! An old evangelist I knew as a boy often used to say, "Believing is the root, feeling is the fruit." This expresses it well.

19. "*Sometimes I fear that I've sinned away my day of grace, for although I've been seeking the Lord for a long time, I don't seem to find Him.*"

No one has sinned away their day of grace if they have any desire to be saved. That desire is divinely implanted. If you are seeking after God it is because He is seeking after you.

But, what, after all, do you really mean when you talk of seeking the Lord and being unable to find Him? He is not hiding Himself. He has come in love to sinners as the good Shepherd seeking the lost sheep.

A little boy was asked one day, "My lad, have you found Jesus?" He looked up in amazement and replied, "Why, sir, I didn't know He was lost, but *I* was, and He found *me*." A wonderful confession surely!

In Old Testament times God said through the prophet, "*Seek the Lord while He may be found; call upon Him while He is near*" (Isaiah 5:6). There is a sense in which these words are still applicable, but they do not convey the full truth of the gospel. Jesus said, *"The Son of Man has come to seek and to save that which was lost"* (Luke 19:10).

Are you lost? Then He is looking for you. *"Do not fear! Stand by and see the salvation of the Lord which He will accomplish for you today"* (Exodus 14:13). Stop right where you are and lift your heart to Him as a repentant sinner, and you will find He is waiting and ready to receive you.

As to sinning away your day of grace, has He not said, *"Whoever will call on the name of the Lord will be saved"* (Romans 8:13). Are *you* not included in that great word *"whoever"*? Unless you can *prove* that it does not include you, you are still where the grace of God can reach you.

Do not listen to the lying voice of the enemy of your soul, who tells you that your case is hopeless. But heed the gentle invitation of Him who is the Way, the Truth, and the Life, as He bids you now believe on His name.

20. *"But how can I be sure that my faith is strong enough to save my soul?"*

It is not *faith* that saves the soul. It is the One who God has set out as the object of faith. It is true we are justified by faith instrumentally, but actually we are justified by His blood. The weakest faith in Jesus saves.

The strongest faith in self, or in good works, or in the church, or in its ordinances leaves you lost and undone still.

James Parker of Plainfield, N. J., was visiting in a hospital, when a nurse indicated a bed surrounded with white screens, and whispered, "The poor man is dying. The priest has been here and administered the last sacrament. He cannot live long."

Mr. Parker begged to go inside the screen, and permission was granted. As he looked down on the dying man he observed a crucifix on his chest. He stooped over and lifted it up.

The sick man lifted his eyes and looked distressed. "Put it back," he whispered, "I want to die with it on my chest."

The visitor pointed to the figure pictured on the cross, and said fervently, "He's a wonderful Savior!"

"Yes, yes, I love the crucifix. Put it back, please. I hope it will help me to die well."

"Not the crucifix," was the reply, "but the One who died on the cross, the Lord Jesus, He died to save you."

The man looked bewildered, then his face brightened: "Oh, I see, not the crucifix but the One who died. He died for me. I see, sir, I see. I never understood it before."

It was evident that faith had sprung up in his soul. Mr. Parker replaced the crucifix, offered a brief prayer, and left. In a few minutes he observed the body being wheeled out of the ward.

Telling me of it later, he exclaimed, "I knew that God thinks so much of the work of His Son that He will have everyone in heaven who will give Him any excuse for taking them there!"

It is blessedly true. Faith's look at the Crucified saves, even though it is faith of the feeblest kind.

21. *"But don't I have to keep God's Law in order to be saved?"*

Keep the Law! Why, you have already violated those sacred precepts times without number. Go carefully over the Ten Commandments. Which of them have you not broken, either literally or in spirit?

Take them one by one, and face them squarely and honestly in the presence of the God who gave them, and who said, "*Moses writes that the man who practices the righteousness which is based on law shall live by that righteousness*" (Romans 10:5); but who also declared, "*For as many as are of the works of the Law are under a curse; for it is written, "Cursed is everyone who does not abide by all things written in the book of the law, to perform them*"(Galatians 3:10).

Let us consider the Ten Commandments seriously. Possibly you will find, by careful examination, that you are not guilty on *every* count of these Ten Commandments. But remember what the Holy Spirit has told us in James 2:8-10: "*If, however, you are fulfilling the royal law according to the Scripture, "You shall love your neighbor as yourself," you are doing well. But if you show partiality, you are committing sin and are convicted by the law as transgressors. For whoever keeps the whole law and yet stumbles in one point, he has become guilty of all.*"

1. You shall have no other gods before Me.

2. You shall not make for yourself an idol... You shall not worship them nor serve them.

3. You shall not take the name of the Lord your God in vain.

4. Remember the Sabbath day, to keep it holy.

5. Honor your father and your mother.

6. You shall not murder.

7. You shall not commit adultery.

8. You shall not steal.

9. You shall not give false testimony against your neighbor.

10. You shall not covet.

It has often been remarked that a chain is no stronger than its weakest link. Suppose you were suspended over a precipice by a chain of ten links. How many would need to snap before you would drop into the abyss below? And so, if you are guilty of the violation of one of the Commandments, you are condemned by the Law and therefore under its curse.

The Law of God was never given to save men. It was given to magnify sin, to make it exceedingly sinful, to give it the specific character of transgression. *"Because by the works of the Law no flesh will be justified in His sight; for through the Law comes the knowledge of sin"* (Romans 3:20).

But, blessed be God, *"Christ redeemed us from the curse of the Law, having become a curse for us – for it is written, 'Cursed is everyone who hangs on a tree'"* (Galatians 3:13). Jesus became man, and was born under the Law. He obeyed that Law perfectly, and was not subject to its penalty. But He went to the cross and endured its curse for us, that we who trust Him might be forever free from its just condemnation.

"He who believes in Him is not judged; he who does not believe has been judged already, because he has not believed in the name of the only begotten Son of God" (John 3:18). *"Therefore there is now no condemnation for those who are in Christ Jesus"* (Romans 8:1).

22. *"But don't I have to first make restitution for all the*

wrongs I have done to other people before I can come to Jesus and be forgiven?"

It is well that you should be concerned as to wrongs done to others, but nowhere in the Word are we told we must make restitution first, though after we are saved we should certainly seek to do all in our power to straighten up any crooked things involving the rights of other people.

It is to those already saved that Paul writes, "*He who steals must steal no longer; but rather he must labor, performing with his own hands what is good, so that he will have something to share with one who has need*" (Ephesians 4:28).

Consider the repentant thief on the cross. Surely he had been guilty of wronging many! Yet the moment he turned in faith to Jesus he was saved. In the very nature of the case he could not make restitution to anyone for any crime committed. His hands and feet were nailed to the cross.

It was not possible for him to do one thing to repair the many wrongs he had done. But through the merits of the Holy Sufferer on that central cross, he was fully and freely pardoned and fitted for Paradise.

Had he been permitted to live and come down from that scaffold, undoubtedly he would have spent his life seeking to show the reality of his repentance, and wherever possible making restitution for offences committed. But he was saved altogether apart from this – on the ground of the full payment for his sins by the Lord Jesus Christ.

You can be saved in the very same way. Then as a new person in Christ, you can prove your love to Him by striving to live unselfishly and devotedly to His glory. And if you are able to put wrongs right, as between man and man, you will in so-doing not only find joy yourself, but you will be a witness to others of the power of saving grace. But all such efforts to clean up the past will have nothing whatever to do with the salvation of your soul. You cannot even help God to save you. It is Jesus Christ's work alone that counts.

23. *"I have a humble hope that I'm a Christian, but I don't dare be too sure. I can't see how anyone can be certain until after the day of judgment."*

But the day of judgment will be too late! If this matter is not settled before that great assize, you will then be permanently lost. Perhaps you are under a misconception of what that judgment of the Great White Throne is for, and who are to be judged at that time. It will be the judgment of sinners, when all who have lived and died without Jesus Christ will be judged according to their works.

Christians will not stand there for judgment. Concerning them our Lord has said (John 5:24): *"Truly, truly, I say to you, he who hears My word, and believes Him who sent Me, has eternal life, and does not come into judgment, but has passed out of death into life."*

Here is a glorious truth revealed! The believers in the Lord Jesus will never have to be judged for their sins, because Jesus has been judged for them already. On account of this, God freely and completely justifies all who receive His Son in faith as their Savior.

Look again at the verse quoted above. Notice that *all* who hear His Word and believe in Him have everlasting life. It is present possession. Therefore it is really unbelief that would lead someone to say, "I *hope* I have eternal life, because I do believe in Jesus." Do not speak of humility when you are doubting God. Take Him at His word and know beyond all question that eternal life is *yours*!

24. *"Don't I have to be baptized before I can know that I'm saved?"*

It is right and proper that you should be baptized. But baptism cannot bring about the salvation of the soul. It is, as Peter tells us, a figure of salvation, just as was the deliverance of Noah in the ark of old. But we are told distinctly, *"For by grace you have been saved through faith; and that not of yourselves, it is the gift of God"* (Ephesians 2:8). To the inquiring jailer at Philippi, who asked the definite question, *"What must I do to be saved?"* there came as definite an answer, *"Believe in the Lord Jesus, and you will be saved"* (Acts 16:30-31).

Baptism followed believing. It was the God-ordained way of confessing Jesus as Savior and Lord. Many have been saved who could not possibly be baptized. Consider again the case of the penitent thief, and be assured that God has never had two ways of saving sinners. The same grace that saved him will save you when you trust in Jesus, whose blood alone cleanses from all sin.

There are a number of passages relating to baptism that can seem a little confusing. But rest your soul on the clear, definite statements concerning salvation by grace, and as you study your Bible the perplexing portions will become clearer under the Holy Spirit's guidance. It is Jesus Christ's baptism of judgment that is the basis of our deliverance from death.

25. *"If I could only be sure I'm in the right church, I would feel secure; but there are so many different churches that I get all confused and upset."*

The Church is not the Ark of Safety. The Church is the aggregate of all who believe in the Lord Jesus, and who have therefore been baptized by the Holy Spirit into one Body. This is not a mere organization, however ancient and venerable. If you were sure you were in the right church (some earthly organization), and trusted in that for salvation, you would be lost forever!

Your trust must be in the Head of the Church, the risen Jesus. He is the *only* Savior. All ecclesiastical pretention is vain, and to trust for salvation through any kind of church membership is an empty deception. Jesus alone is the Ark that will carry you safely through all the storms of judgment. No matter what denomination you turn to, you will never find salvation by allying yourself with it. But when you come to Jesus, you are then prepared to enjoy fellowship with His people.

26. *"I believe that Jesus died for me, but I'm afraid to say that I'm saved, for I know I don't love God as much as I should."*

I question if *anyone* loves God as He ought to be loved. But it is a grave mistake to be looking in your own heart for love. Rather, rejoice in the amazing love of God for you as expressed in the cross of Jesus, and in all His care for you through the years.

We say sometimes that "love begets love." In other words, "If someone behaves lovingly to another person, that person will behave lovingly to them." This is very true in regard to love for God. As you are fully engaged with His love, your own heart will respond to it and you will be able to say, "*We love, because He first loved us*" (1 John 4:19).

Looking into your own heart for a ground of confidence is like dropping the anchor into the hold of a ship. Cast it outside and let it go down, down, down into the great, tossing ocean of strife and trouble, until it grips the Rock itself. Christ alone is the Rock, and He is the foundation of the infinite love of God for sinners.

27. *"At times I feel assured that all is well, but at other times I tremble, fearing that I'm mistaken."*

Mistaken about what? If you believe that Jesus died for you and rose again, there can be no mistake about that. If you have taken Him at His word, and have come to Him for peace and pardon, there can be no mistake about that. If you have opened your heart to Him, you can be certain He has come in to abide, for He has told you He would, and there can be no mistake about that. Your trembling does not alter these basic facts.

A story is told of a vessel that was wrecked one stormy night by crashing on the rocks off the coast of Cornwall. All hands perished but one lone Irish lad, who was hurled by the waves on the jagged slopes of a great towering ledge where he managed to find a place of refuge.

In the morning, watchers on the beach spied him through their glasses, and a boat was launched and rowed out to where he clung.

Almost dead with cold and exposure, he was tenderly lifted into the boat and brought ashore. After restoratives were applied, he was asked, "Lad, didn't you tremble out there on the rock in all that storm?"

He replied brightly, "Tremble? Yes, I trembled. But do you know, the rock never trembled once all night."

If you have trusted Jesus, you are on the Rock. While you may tremble, that does not invalidate God's salvation. The Rock remains firm and secure. Look away from self altogether and rely solely on the Word of God.

> "When darkness veils His lovely face,
> I rest on His unchanging grace;
> In ev'ry high and stormy gale,
> My anchor holds within the veil.
> On Christ, the solid Rock, I stand,
> All other ground is sinking sand."

28. *"There have been times when I've had very definite assurance of my salvation, and then I've have lost it again. Why do these periods of darkness come?"*

There can be various reasons for these periods of darkness. The greatest saints have at times known the same experiences. They can possibly be accounted for by great mental weariness and physical weakness.

The adversary of our souls is always ready to take advantage of such conditions, and it always seeks to make us forget the clear, definite promises of God on which we have rested when well and strong.

There is an authentic story told of an aged minister who had preached the gospel in clearness and power during all his public life, but who, when he was old and suffering from confusion at times, found himself greatly troubled by doubt and uncertainty. Mentioning the matter to his wife, she drew his attention to John 5:24.

As he read the precious words again, "*Truly, truly, I say to you, he who hears My word, and believes Him who sent Me, has eternal life, and does not come into judgment, but has passed out of death into life,*" he burst into a joyous laugh, and said, "How strange that I should ever forget words like these, when I have preached on them myself for years."

Sometime later the wife came into the room and found her aged husband leaning over the side of the bed, holding the open Bible beneath it. She exclaimed, "Whatever are you doing?"

He answered, "Satan has been after me again, and as he is the prince of darkness I took it that he would be in the darkest place in the room, which is under the bed. So I was just showing him John 5:24, and the moment he saw it he ceased to trouble me."

We can quite understand the mental frailty that the story suggests, but the principle is blessedly true. When the adversary of your soul comes against you seeking to destroy your confidence, show him what God has said.

But there can be other reasons which account for the loss of that blessed assurance you once enjoyed. The apostle Peter suggests such in his Second Epistle, chapter 1, verse 9: "*He who lacks these qualities is blind or short-sighted, having forgotten his purification from his former sins.*"

In verses 1-8 we read, "*To those who have received a faith of the same kind as ours, by the righteousness of our God and Savior, Jesus Christ: Grace and peace be multiplied to you in the knowledge of God and of Jesus our Lord; seeing that His divine power has granted to us everything pertaining to life and godliness, through the true knowledge of Him who called us by His own glory and excellence.*

"For by these He has granted to us His precious and magnificent promises, so that by them you may become partakers of the divine nature, having escaped the corruption that is in the world by lust.

"Now for this very reason also, applying all diligence, in your faith supply moral excellence, and in your moral excellence, knowledge, and in your knowledge, self-control, and in your self-control, perseverance, and in your perseverance, godliness, and in your godliness, brotherly kindness, and in your brotherly kindness, love.

"For if these qualities are yours and are increasing, they render you neither useless nor unfruitful in the true knowledge of our Lord Jesus Christ."

But, on the other hand, if the believer is neglectful of these things, he cannot expect the divine blessing to rest on him. As have seen in verse 9, *"He who lacks these qualities is blind or short-sighted, having forgotten his purification from his former sins."*

There is something very solemn here. Notice, he was purified from his old sins, but through laziness and carelessness he has lost the assurance of this. The blessedness of bygone days has faded from his memory.

The Christian life is never static. One must either grow in grace, or there will be backsliding and deterioration. *"The backslider in heart will have his fill of his own ways, but a good man will be satisfied with his"* (Proverbs 14:14). The person who does not go on with God, but allows themselves to drift, is almost sure to lose the joy of their salvation.

Examine yourself as to this matter, and if you find that you have been careless in regard to the study of your Bible, careless as to your prayer life, careless as to the proper use of the means of grace, confess all this to God and give diligence to walk with Him in days to come, that you can develop a stronger Christian character.

Last of all, let me remind you that any known sin condoned in your life will rob you of the joy and assurance of your salvation. "*If I regard wickedness in my heart, the Lord will not hear*" (Psalm 66:18).

Many a one who has gone on happily with Jesus for some time, but through toying with sin has become ensnared and entrapped into something that has so grieved the Spirit of God that they have lost their sense of acceptance in Jesus. We must see to it that there is no unconfessed sin in our life. Be sure that we are not tolerating any secret sin.

Do not accept the suggestion of the tempter that you are powerless to break away from evil habits. Remember, it is not a question of your own power, but when you honestly repent of the wrong-doing and turn to the Lord for divine help to overcome your sin, He will undertake for you.

As you reckon yourself to be dead indeed to sin, but alive to God through Jesus Christ our Lord, the Holy Spirit will work in and through you, causing you to triumph over tendencies toward evil, enabling you to live victoriously to the glory of the God who has saved you.

Epilogue

Now, I realize that your particular difficulty may not have been touched at all in the preceding pages. But whatever it is that keeps you from the positive assurance that your soul is saved, I beg of you not to give up in despair and conclude that such knowledge is not for you. For whatever your condition of mind, whatever your trouble of conscience, whatever your particular troublesome sin may be, there is that in God's holy Word which is designed to exactly meet your case.

Will you not definitely settle it with God that you will take the Lord Jesus Christ as your own personal Savior, and then, in dependence on the Holy Spirit, search the Scriptures daily, reading prayerfully and thoughtfully, and look up to God Himself for all needed enlightenment? *"He leads the humble in justice, and He teaches the humble His way"* (Psalm 25:9). Again, He says, *"To this one I will look, to him who is humble and contrite of spirit, and who trembles at My word"* (Isaiah 66:2).

Our blessed Lord has declared that if anyone is willing to do the will of God, all that is needed is to come in humility of mind and contrition of heart, counting on God who is not willing that any should perish, to reveal His mind to you through the written Word, thus leading on to the assurance of peace with God through Jesus Christ.

But, on the other hand, do not be neglectful of the

means of grace He has put at your disposal. If you are so placed that you can hear the ministry of the Word, go as often as you can to hear the gospel proclaimed, for when the world by its wisdom does not know God, "*God was well-pleased through the foolishness of the message preached to save those who believe*" (1 Corinthians 1:21).

Frequent, too, the place of prayer, and be ready to consult with others who give evidence of knowing and enjoying what you are seeking. It was when Lydia was at the place of prayer that Paul was sent to explain the way of life, and the Lord opened her heart to receive it. She was earnestly seeking in accordance with all the light she had, and the Lord saw to it that more light came as she followed the gleam (Acts 16:11-15).

Another thing is very important for anyone desiring divine illumination: Put out of your life every known sin, so far as it is in your power to do so, and avoid all that would tend to defile your mind and heart. Remember the words of David, we read earlier. "*If I regard wickedness in my heart, the Lord will not hear*" (Psalm 66:18).

If you continue to associate needlessly with the ungodly, or if you participate in ungodly matters which have a tendency to harden the conscience, you cannot expect to get help from the Spirit of God, who is grieved by all such questionable activities.

Do not waste precious time on unhelpful literature. Give the first place to your Bible, and make use of any good books that you are able to obtain – books that enlighten and make eternal things more real. It is folly to expect the assurance of salvation, and yet neglect the means that God has ordained for making known the riches of His grace.

"In Him we have redemption through His blood, the forgiveness of our trespasses, according to the riches of His grace (Ephesians 1:7).

Rock of Ages, cleft for me,
Let me hide myself in Thee;
Let the water and the blood,
From Thy wounded side which flowed,
Be of sin the double cure;
Cleanse me from its guilt and power.

Not the labor of my hands
Can fulfill Thy law's demands;
Could my zeal no respite know,
Could my tears forever flow,
All for sin could not atone;
Thou must save, and Thou alone.

Nothing in my hand I bring,
Simply to Thy cross I cling;
Naked, come to Thee for dress;
Helpless look to Thee for grace;
Foul, I to the Fountain fly;
Wash me, Savior, or I die.

While I draw this fleeting breath,
When mine eyelids close in death
When I soar to worlds unknown,
See Thee on Thy judgment throne,
Rock of Ages, cleft for me,
Let me hide myself in Thee.

About White Tree Publishing

White Tree Publishing publishes mainstream evangelical Christian literature for people of all ages, with over 200 titles available. We aim to make our eBooks available free for all eBook devices, but some distributors will only list our books free at their discretion, and may make a small charge for some titles – but they are still great value!

All our books are fully typeset. No "photocopies" or bad OCR! Long sentences and paragraphs are broken into shorter lengths, and modern punctuation is used for easier reading. Many books are sensitively abridged.

There are over 200 books listed on our website, arranged under the names of Christian nonfiction authors, Christian fiction authors, and Christian books for younger readers, both fiction and nonfiction.

Please let your friends and your church leaders know about our books – and also Christian TV and radio broadcasters.

https://whitetreepublishing.com/

Lightning Source UK Ltd.
Milton Keynes UK
UKHW021831060522
402557UK00006B/168